ITA FORD: MISSIONARY MARTYR

PHYLLIS ZAGANO

PAULIST PRESS
New York / Mahwah, N.J.

The Publisher acknowledges the use of selected texts and letters from:
Ita Ford, M.M. Letters. *Same Fate as the Poor* Collection. Maryknoll Sisters
Archives. Maryknoll Mission Archives. Maryknoll, New York. Used by permission of the Maryknoll Sisters of St. Dominic, Inc., Maryknoll, N.Y. All rights
reserved.

Transcriptions of selected texts and letters of Ita Ford by Phyllis Zagano.

Cover design by Cindy Dunne.

Cover photo courtesy of William P. Ford.

Library of Congress Cataloging-in-Publication Data

Zagano, Phyllis.
    Ita Ford : missionary martyr / Phyllis Zagano.
       p.   cm.
    ISBN 0-8091-3663-5 (alk. paper)
    1. Ford, Ita, d. 1980.   2. Maryknoll Sisters—Latin America—Biography.
3. Missionaries—Latin America—Biography.   4. Christian martyrs—El
Salvador—Biography. I. Title.
BV2300.M4Z34   1996
266′.2′092—dc20
[B]   96-5523
                                                             CIP

Published by Paulist Press
997 Macarthur Boulevard
Mahwah, New Jersey 07430

Printed and bound in the
United States of America

For the ones we don't know about

PREFACE

People always ask why you wrote this article or that book, and I suppose it is useful to try to answer, but in this case I have to say I am not sure. That is, I am not sure what it was about Ita Ford that resounded within me.

I can tell you that I found out about her when I read about her in *The New York Times* in early December, 1980, and realized that some fools in El Salvador had raped and killed four women missionaries, but that is not how I got to know Ita Ford.

I "met" her first through a Maryknoll publication—-a small card with her photograph and a quote from her letter to her niece: "I hope you come to find that which gives life a deep meaning for you. Something worth living for— maybe even worth dying for…." Both the card and that sentiment stayed a long time with me, and when I was preparing *Woman to Woman: An Anthology of Women's Spiritualities* (The Liturgical Press, 1993) I went to the Maryknoll Archives to learn more about Ita Ford.

There is no preparation for encountering such a soul. I learned, and I continue to learn, about a genuinely good woman who truly lived as best she was able the life God laid out for her. Not all of it was her choice; not all of it was happy. All of it was lived joyfully in God's care.

I am still learning about Ita Ford; I want to write more about her. At this point, I can thank and thank deeply those who have shared both their time and their memories and, while she would never impose such an order (or any order) on her many friends and relatives and acquaintances, those whom I have met so far here stand alphabetically side by side: Madeline Dorsey, MM, William P. Ford, Harry Gaffney, Kate Monahan Gregg, M. Edmund Harvey, RSHM, Peggy Healy, Mary Lou Herlihy, MM, Camilla Kennedy, MM, Grace Krieger, MM, Alfonse Ligouri, Beverly Malone, Janice McLaughlin, MM, Anna Mammana May, Grace Myerjack, MM, Grace Monahan Niemeyer, and Rose Tocci.

Thanks go as well to those who helped with research and translation: past and present staff of the Boston University Libraries and of the Maryknoll Archives, and Ana Ballester, Rene Duran, Antonio de las Morenas, M.D., Grace Krieger, MM, Brinsley Horner, Lorette Larkin, CSJ, Janice McLaughlin, MM, Virginia McKenna, RSHM, Phillip Redman, Teresa Rorke, CSJ, Raphael Velasquez, and Elizabeth Yakel;

to those who helped with final editing: James A. Brann and Kate Monahan Gregg;

to those whose research I used in the Maryknoll Archives: Judith Noone, MM, and Maureen Flanagan;

to those friends who walked with me as I began to walk with Ita, including Irene Kelly, RSHM, and Carolyn O'Hara, OCD;

and to Kathleen Walsh at Paulist Press.

All have helped me to correct my mistakes, and only I may have neglected to do so.

New York, October 18, 1995

I truly believe that I should be here and I can't even tell you why....God's palpable presence has never been more real ever since we came to Salvador—He's made a lot of things clear to us—what we should be doing, etc.—and I trust in that and I hope you can too.

—Ita Ford, September 7, 1980

INTRODUCTION

This life ended with a bullet in the brain.

At approximately 10:30 p.m. on December 2, 1980, Maryknoll Sister Ita Ford, having been abducted, stripped and brutalized, was shot in the back of the head by one of the following men: Luis Antonio Colindres Aleman, 25; Carlos Joaquin Contreras Palacios, 23; Francisco Orlando Contreras Recinos, 31; Jose Roberto Moreno Canjura, 24; Daniel Canales Ramirez, 23.

She was in El Salvador with three other American missionaries: Ursuline Sister Dorothy Kazel, Maryknoll Sister Maura Clarke, and Jean Donovan. Each was shot, and left uncovered and undressed. They were buried the next day in a common grave by local farmers.

Carlos Joaquin Contreras Palacios, the youngest, confessed. He tried later to explain that the women disrobed and submitted voluntarily, and that they had subversive propaganda with them. He, like the others, was a member of the Salvadoran National Guard.

These are the facts of the deaths. This is about Ita Ford's life.

I.

It was cool and cloudy when Ita Ford was born in Brooklyn, on April 23, 1940. Her parents, Mildred Teresa O'Beirne and William Patrick Ford, had been born in this century to the promise of middle-class American life: she became the sort of New York City public school teacher who could "teach a carrot to read," he the genteel insurance agent, full of Irish song and wit.

Ita's brother, Bill, preceded her; her sister, Rene, came after. Together they endured "a Board of Education diet—wheat germ on everything" along with the usual constellation of big brother–middle sister–little sister consternations. Ita was always small—sometimes slight, sometimes chubby—by high school about 5'2" with the sort of build that causes yearbook editors to write "pixie" as part of the description. All her schooling was the white-glove Catholic of the 1950s and 1960s: Visitation Academy and The Fontbonne Hall Academy in Bay Ridge. Ita was assistant editor of her high school paper, editor of her college yearbook. At twenty-one she received a baccalaureate degree in English from Marymount Manhattan College, a small, Catholic commuter school on New York's Upper East Side.

Well before that she began to dream of missionary life. Early in her sophomore year in college she first contacted the Maryknoll Sisters of St. Dominic in Ossining, New York. She wrote to her friend Jean Baumann: "I've acquired a preliminary questionnaire for Maryknoll & I expect to go up there Christmas week to look the place over....I'm doing my level best to make this thing work for next September."

It did not. Medical tests (her father had had tuberculosis) and Maryknoll's own determinations delayed her. Not incidentally, her mother remained unconvinced. Ita kept trying and found herself third time lucky, finally accepted for entrance in 1961. In the meanwhile, she had matured to "a new set of values" recognized after a senior-year trip to Russia: "It was the idea that these people...who really deserved freedom of religion—they were the ones denied it. It was pathetic and nauseating at the same time...[and] made me aware now that I really have to go to Maryknoll."

II.

Ita Catherine Ford entered Maryknoll in August, 1961, one of sixty-four young women endeavoring to learn missionary life. A postulant mistress of the time recalls her as "sophisticated"—a graduate of a "special" college, a gifted and acute observer who raised questions to the point of challenge. While Ita was not ordinarily allowed home visits, the postulant mistress remembers traveling with her on the New York subways heading for a family funeral in Brooklyn. With an eye for detail and a delight in the city around her, Ita pointed out the unique mosaics for each station—the beavers at Astor Place, for example—to the St. Louis native who accompanied her.

But her entry into religious life was difficult in many ways. She wrote: "It's lonely. Not in [the] sense of being alone in a crowd, but in an emotional way. No one knows you well enough to be able to say the right thing when you need it—and as yet, no one cares enough." The pain of separation waned as friendships formed, and her detachment from things material (but not from things intellectual) grew as the first year went on. She complained about the classes, and feared intellectual stagnation. In another letter she wrote: "...now I really don't mind having few belongings—it simplifies things—in fact I never thought a 3rd pair of shoes could be superfluous—now yes!"

A healthy detachment, and a deep understanding of what is known as poverty of spirit, are basic to religious life, and the process of letting go is lifelong. "Making" the stations of the cross, by meditating on the fourteen final events in the life and death of Jesus, often brings one to these points. Ita wrote her friend: "I'm not much of a station maker but one day during Lent I was thinking about it— and I was particularly struck by the tenth one. What could be harder than being stripped not of your clothes—but of all that goes to make you up, and yet what was more necessary than that very thing? Somehow you have to peel off all the layers you've acquired, all those things that go to hinder you when you really want to make the break. It fascinated me. I could see so many things that had to go—and still have to, if I was to get anywhere."

III.

The "stripping" required for a mature interior life should be a carefully monitored process. Maryknoll's novitiate, like others, could have added its own bureaucracy to the confusing time of preparation and of trial. Ita was never a fan of bureaucracy in any form; she wrote: "If anything could ruin your life, it's the petty daily stupidities—that so distract you from the all important."

Her early years at Maryknoll could not have been easy. She was a little older than the others, although by far not the eldest. She was more educated than most, and so she found the classes repetitive; she ached for copies of *The New Yorker* and almost anything else that would have stirred her literary mind. Her movement toward missionary life required a self-donation that the world generally does not understand, something she found hard to describe at first. She wrote about life within Maryknoll: "Even just to have a knowledge of the love that exists inside, and the reality of the relationship you can have with God....I am at a complete loss as how to explain this to anyone who thinks this is a waste of time."

She chafed at some things, excelled at others, and hung on. She was widely and well liked by the other novices. Still, the novitiate in Topsfield, Massachusetts became a pressure cooker for Ita. Another novice recalls that it seemed some were asked to leave suddenly, without reason or warning. The slips of paper in the mailboxes inevitably increased the

11

tensions in the house, especially as the time for first vows drew near. Ita was worried—she wanted this so very much—and feared she would be the next to go. For whatever reason, she developed a "nervous stomach," and her initial medical evaluation could have blamed the stress of having to prove herself. Her first vows were temporarily delayed; she wrote to her friend: "My stomach has been on the skitz, and last Monday the doctor asked that I not be under the pressure of taking vows on the 24th."

The reprieve was short-lived, and the decision made final two months later: "I'm home—Wednesday afternoon it was official that I couldn't take vows....It's a shock and disappointment and I don't think I'm operating on all engines but I'll bounce soon."

IV.

There is a particular emotional danger for anyone asked to leave religious life, and the risk of imagining a "rejection by God" needs to be addressed quickly. However reluctantly religious orders might send someone away, a life's plan remains ruptured. While Ita's apparent physical condition would have ruled out her serving in foreign missions in the early 1960s (or today), Maryknoll was the only vocation she ever knew. Her dream was foreclosed in August, 1964, and she could not understand what happened, or why. She landed at LaGuardia bewildered, and went home to Brooklyn.

There was no hope of returning to Maryknoll, but there seems no embarrassment about her situation in her letters. Maryknoll had provided her with counseling before she left; she traveled to meet an additional six to eight times with the same woman psychiatrist until, as she put it, she decided she could have lunch a lot cheaper in New York than in Boston.

Ita also kept in touch with her truly compassionate novice mistress, Sister Paul Miriam: "It's four weeks since I arrived home, and though it's still very unreal, I am getting settled. Through Marymount I got a position at Sadlier Text Books, doing editorial work on a new series of High School English books. This is not completely new for I had been on the staff of the newspaper and yearbook. For right now it seems the best thing to do." She must have been encouraged to get involved with some sort of church work—she taught religious education classes part-time at a poor parish in lower Manhattan and reported back on her experiences: "Theoretically, I teach C.C.D., but I never teach any topic at all. They were supposed to be studying the commandments but they hardly know the basic prayers. Though Sunday mass isn't too high on their priority lists, they do have a wonderful Christian attitude toward each other. I guess that's why I love them."

V.

Ita continued to fall in love—with her friends, with her work, with her life, and with a young Japanese-American lawyer whom she perhaps thought she would marry.

She was an immediately likeable person, totally forthright and agreeable. When Harry Gaffney hired her at Sadlier she told him she left Maryknoll because she did not have the physical resources for missionary life. He recalls her as small but not sickly, one of many young, bright, articulate Catholics at the company. Sadlier's editorial department socialized a great deal, their closeness generated by an office layout that guaranteed constant contact. One former colleague, Beverly Malone, recalls Ita routinely showing up around 5:00 p.m. at her office door: "Now?" came the question from behind a cloud of Kent cigarette smoke. And now it was, as they went downstairs to the Parker House for an hour of smokes and scotch and food and gab before returning to work.

Happy memories pour out of Ita's friends even today. In fact, no one seems to be able to speak about Ita Ford without smiling. Most recall her as shy, but with something to say—a "true renaissance woman"—and not incidentally the smartest woman any of the men had ever met. She was a delight at a party, and always delighted to be there.

It was a time in New York history when a slight, brown-haired, left-handed, 26-year-old woman could drink Dewar's and water, and smoke a pack or two a day, and be happy doing what she was doing without burrow-ing along a career path. She socialized, she took courses at Hunter College, and she enjoyed New York. Eventually Ita moved from her parents' Brooklyn home to wonderful New York, New York, to an apartment close to Greenwich Village, in Sheridan Square.

Still at Sadlier, Ita became a trusted editor, first work-ing on a twelve-volume high school literature program called "Structure in Language and Literature," then as an editor of religious texts, and involved in the earliest Sadlier audio-visual productions. Her co-workers recall her lively cynicism and friendly liberal attitude; she was politically informed, somewhat politically active, and non-partisan in her politics. Dead set like the others against the war in Vietnam, she still did not attend a huge peace rally at City Hall Park.

Ita's reactions to political questions were predictably unpredictable. A California priest-author and friend recalled sightseeing in New York with her: "Ita had a criti-cal mind, non-ideological; even in the mid-sixties we met a fellow taking signatures to stop the building of a nuclear power plant, and Ita challenged the guy to tell us where New York would get power if they didn't build the plant. She said she would think it over before she signed."

As months stretched into years, Maryknoll faded, but she kept up a lively correspondence with her former sisters, now around the world.

VI.

Meeting up in New York with her Maryknoll friends
was easier after Ita moved into the two-bedroom
apartment in Sheridan Square. Soon her roommate was her
high school and college friend Kathy Monahan, and they
did what young women did in New York City in 1970, and
had a wonderful time of it.

Kathy Monahan recalls living with Ita: she was an
incredibly healthy eater ("peas? fish?"), she enjoyed many
and varied friendships, and she spent long, long hours keep-
ing up a voluminous correspondence with Maryknollers. In
retrospect, although she was away, Maryknoll never really
left Ita, and her extended community of friends circled the
globe. Neither did she ever decide that marriage was for her.
As her relationship with the lawyer ended, she continued to
go out with her college crowd, which increasingly included
husbands.

There were trips with Kathy Monahan and Anna
Mammana: to Provincetown, where they sat on the rocks
and talked away half the night; to California and
Disneyland, where the ticket seller offered Anna a reduced
ticket for her "child"; to Mexico, where they stayed in
cheap places and climbed the wall of a fancy hotel to swim
in the pool. Letters from Ita's father, words woven into a
bright tapestry of memories and presence, arrived at the
local Hilton each stop along the way. She shared them, she
kept them, she had them in El Salvador the night she died.

Words were important, and Ita was deliberate with them. Her own careful writing belied the fact that it took some time for her to be as precise in speech. She did not speak much in a group, but when she spoke, it was either the funniest or the deepest comment the whole night long.

She also kept her own counsel, and when she announced in 1971 that she was returning to Maryknoll, her friends were both surprised and half expecting it. Ita was not looking for a spectacular life. She simply wished to live and work as a missionary among the poor.

Harry Gaffney recalls her appearing in his office door one day at Sadlier: "I'm leaving," she said. He rushed to counter any offer the competition could have made, but there was no contest. "Maryknoll finally accepted me," she said.

VII.

First she went to St. Louis.

She wrote to a friend: "In the area in which we live, which in my yet not-too-clear sense of direction seems kind of in the middle of the city, I get a strange feeling of one-time opulence. The houses are large stone, three-storey affairs, fit for comfortable burghers at the beginning of the century. Some have turrets and others interesting architectural features. Now I'm sure they are subdivided into apartments, but from the street, you still get a sense of stability, roots, large families, etc."

She was ten years older and ten pounds lighter when she went to Missouri for her second Maryknoll novitiate. Since she had already completed a "canonical year," after seven months or so she was invited to temporary profession as a Maryknoll Sister. On April 29, 1972 she publicly made a Promise of Fidelity "to live poverty, obedience and celibate love in community, according to the gospel counsels and the constitutions of the Maryknoll Sisters until the time of my final commitment." Her Topsfield novice mistress, Sister Paul Miriam, attended the ceremony.

Whatever was left open eight years before was now definitively closed; with the help of God and Maryknoll she had regained her sense of self: "…if we can be ourselves & accept ourselves…obviously limited, weak, imperfect—& accept the mysterious fact that we are loveable—not in spite of ourselves but as we are….You can be

who you are—and become more. I know this is true
because it happened to me. Who I am now is due to many
people who cared for me and those who do now." Her St.
Louis novice mistress recalls her as "so ordinary, you'd
miss her." She fit in that perfectly.

While at St. Louis Ita gained new friends whose cur-
rent insights to her personality mirror those with longer
knowledge of her: all who knew Ita on a personal level saw
that she had suffered deeply in her life. It was not easy for
her to leave Maryknoll, and it was not easy for her to decide
to go back. One sister remembers: "She was intense, intelli-
gent and extremely sensitive—and her search was to find
meaning in her life—to live a life that made sense—and she
found it with Maryknoll."

From St. Louis Ita headed toward language studies in
Bolivia, attempting stops along the way to visit with other
Maryknoll Sisters. "Of course, most of the travel depends on
the weather. It will be the rainy season—during which roads,
bridges, etc. often disappear in mudslides or become impas-
sible—so we'll see." She eventually made her way to the
Institute de Idomas at Cochabamba, Bolivia to learn
Spanish—a task both arduous and hilarious, and which also
introduced her first-hand to the ingenious ways missionaries
have of passing mail along to friends and families. She
inquired about one package, explaining its circuitous routing
back to Brooklyn: "Down here you'd think Maryknoll was a
competing postal system. No one goes anywhere without
mail and packages. We even call it a 'would you mind'."

As the "would you minds" continued, Ita was able to
report on her possible assignment in a politically tense Chile:

"I am just back in Santiago after roaming around the central portion of the country for seven weeks during which I was supposedly getting some brief idea of what is going on and how Maryknoll is relating to it. I think what happened was that I just got very confused and tired. What happens next is still somewhat up in the air....I'm to be thinking where I go next for a period of in-service training....Some people say I couldn't have come at a more exciting time while others say this is a terrible introduction. I guess that's indicative of what's going on." As Ita began to see the poverty of the people, she began as well to see the purpose of her presence among them. Soon she settled with other Maryknoll Sisters in one of the many squatters' shantytowns that ring Santiago, first in Poblacion Manuel Rodriguez, then in Poblacion La Bandera. "Home is a small wooden house with three bedrooms and a living-dining-kitchen. Also indoor plumbing. It's comfortable and simple....What we hope to be doing here is building community among ourselves, and establishing relationships with some of the people. Just what form that will take for me I still don't know....Because of the history and tradition of the people, there is not much of an emphasis on sacramentalization or other institutional works. Rather it is the hope of the bishop of the area that through developing relations with the people there will slowly evolve a small base Christian community that reflects and prays together. Worship comes later."

When she explained her life to her friends, she described simple presence: "What am I doing? I amble around the poblacion at a very leisurely rate—and if someone looks receptive, I say hello and try some conversation.

Or I go home visiting for a clinic nearby to check up on the babies who haven't been brought for the monthly control. Or I go to meetings or sit in on some adult education classes—women who never finished 8 years and are now in a gov't program to get finished. I also wait on lines—to get food, kerosene or whatever." Her life was to suffer with the people, with the Church: one day planted weapons were found in a tabernacle, and the military detained the priest and searched the entire area. The bishop denounced the whole event as a sham. Her own life churned in the balance: "The tension between Church and state helps keep us all honest. You have to make decisions, even though they won't be popular and can easily be twisted. So we muddle along." She admitted that the kinds of things the Church chose to do and the kinds of things the Church could do were mere temporary measures, because "the Church cannot, should not, take on responsibilities that belong to organized government."

The Maryknoll Sisters ran a mental health clinic for the women of the area. Chile had eighty psychiatrists for the million or so people the World Health Organization said suffered from neuroses at the time, primarily due to the six-year siege of economically disabling military rule. What moved Ita most deeply was the pain of individuals who together comprised a country of poor sufferers, whom she viewed through the faith she sought to share: "I see Chile deeply experiencing the paschal mystery, with the light of Easter still to come…the cup cannot pass without our drinking it."

VIII.

It is difficult to listen to Ita Ford's taped recollections of life in Chile.

The Chilean rule "disappeared" men whose lives and voices became troublesome and made the job complete by destroying their records: they never existed. The wives of the "disappeared" had two choices: they could complain of what happened and risk economic ostracism, or lie that their scoundrel husbands abandoned them, and so get jobs to feed their children. Relief supplies were so scarce the sisters had to weigh the children who came to them, carrying their spoons (there was no money for utensils); those who had gained normal weight were turned away so others could take their places.

Much of what Ita and the others did—could do—was simply be present to the poor. These poor of Chile had perhaps one meal per day; their children saved their milk rations to share with those at home. Once a man said to Ita: "The Church has changed....Before, we had to go up to the Church. Now it's the Church that comes to us." Finding her place in the sacramental, rite-oriented Church, Ita called her work similar to that of a Protestant pastor: "caring, being concerned about, being involved in the lives" of the people. Her frustration was with "the temporary measures that don't touch the source of the problem. At best, they serve as a means of denouncing a situation of sin and injustice."

While Ita had a careful appreciation of the political situations that led to the suffering of the people around her, she did not readily articulate the solutions in political terms. Her ministry was to those affected, independent of cause or reason, and primarily to aid them in resolving their dilemmas. She wrote of her caring for the women and the children especially: "Working with the poor calls for a great restraint and modesty on all levels so as not to overpower, overcome or take over the situation. It certainly has been a great advantage working in La Bandera...a modest presence. There's no church 'plant'; there's no power structure. There's nothing to protect or defend. Money coming for projects such as the dining rooms is channeled through the deanery or zone to be pooled among the other poblaciones of the area."

It was a Church of the poor for the poor, which she saw as credible. For her, "being with the poor means overcoming our distaste of getting dirty literally and metaphorically: the literal dirt, mud, excrement; caring for and supporting the sinner, the underdog, and unpopular causes; entering into messed-up lives; running the risk of being misunderstood, misinterpreted, of being accused as subversives, etc."

Her modest presence made a distinct difference in many lives.

IX.

Progress is often mere persistence.

After six years in Chile, as life within the poblacion deepened, Ita was asked to return to Maryknoll for a "Reflection Year" in preparation for final vows. She tried to postpone, but came as called in the fall of 1978.

She had a missionary's reaction to the abundance of the United States. She still delighted in the people at parties, but the food piled high troubled her; she walked into a party at Sadlier and remarked she could feed her whole poblacion with that spread. She made the rounds of friends, and each noted a new reticence, a new sensitivity. Her repeated falls and consistent compassion for others combined to instill an even deeper sense of self and of the needs of others, perhaps tempered with a bit of embarrassment at her own frailties.

Missionary life is difficult; it was for her, it is for others. At some point the reality crashes in: there is no limit to what is required. She wrote mid-way through her Reflection Year: "One day at mass here the words of the consecration went booming through me—this is my body given for you. The connection was instantaneous—all those giving their bodies—the possibilities there are for us to give our bodies—it was all made so possible & powerful—Jesus' having given his because he loved."

The connection between what happened to her and the love of God was not always that apparent. "Why?" was the enduring question of her life. She was not all that enthusiastic about a year in New York, after the depth and breadth of her missionary experience in Chile. There were four others who shared her Reflection Year; each was in preparation for final vows and none particularly wanted to be in Ossining. They chose to live in the large Maryknoll Sisters' complex, rather than separate themselves off in a small house together, and found grand friendships within and without their little band.

It did not matter that she wished she were someplace else. Ita could still enjoy life. She loved to dance. She loved a good time. She would often meet another sister in a television lounge late on a Saturday night, and the two would scream laughing at "Saturday Night Live."

Typically clad in blue jeans and a plaid blouse, she made it through the Reflection Year. She bounded toward the door for Memorial Day weekend and a few days in Rhode Island, then to Massachusetts with friends before her return to Chile. The call came back to Maryknoll: there had been an accident and Ita, only Ita, was hurt. Fractured pelvis, damaged knee. Why? The question ricocheted around her head as days turned into weeks and months and still her leg needed strengthening. Why? She weighted her ankle with rocks and exercised in the kitchen of the Sisters' vacation house in Watch Hill, Rhode Island, and spoke of people and their needs in places distant: Chile, Zimbabwe, Mozambique. Why? She needed, she wanted, so much to return to Chile, to the people who had no respite from being poor.

As 1979 turned into 1980, she got back to Chile, and started looking for something to do.

X.

The needs of the Church suffering are often articulated by the Church hierarchical, and 1978–1979 brought multiple fractures to Central and South America. The new call came from Nicaragua, and from El Salvador. Again war, again repression, again so many poor, so many refugees. The Byzantine politics of the region were all the more complicated by American assistance.

While Nicaragua had gained some semblance of peace, El Salvador was a cauldron. Throughout this century, fourteen extended families comprised the oligarchy whose interests were protected by the military they controlled. In the early 1960s political parties began to form, and accusations and deaths continued to boil over until a 1979 coup put Colonel Napolean Duarte in power. San Salvador's Archbishop Oscar Romero called for help: guerrillas from various groups were training and hiding in the three-mile demilitarized zone created to maintain the peace along the Honduras border. Their activities, and the forays of their enemies to extinguish them, created refugees who had to walk south, away from what little they had.

For many, the Salvadoran military and National Guard were indistinguishable from the death squads rooting out supporters of the Revolutionary Democratic Front (FDR), the Farabundo Martí National Liberation Front (FMLN), and other, smaller groups. The American Embassy's political section believed that the death squads were "ad hoc vigilante groups that coalesce according to perceived need" although, the Embassy official wrote, "security force members utilize the guise of the death squad when a potentially embarrassing or odious task needs to be performed."

With these wounds, Salvador became a possibility for Maryknoll missionary effort. Ita wrote to her mother: "...after meetings in different countries, it's now been decided that Nicaragua & Salvador—for different reasons—are both congregational priorities for Latin America. As a person between jobs at this point, I've had to look at that priority & say I'm open to consider it. Right now, there are meetings going on in Salvador to establish priorities & job descriptions....In some ways, there's no difference between the needs of Chile & Salvador—there's plenty of work to be done in both. What even makes Salvador a question is the congregation's seeing that it's very important at this time to support Archbishop Romero...."

Ita responded. If the suffering was caused by one or another political situation, it did not matter. The creation of suffering, the creation of need and want and death by individuals marked sinful situations that needed to be addressed by the Church present. So within a few months— from November, 1979 to April, 1980—Ita Ford traveled from Ossining to Nicaragua, to Chile and back to Nicaragua and, finally, in Easter Week, 1980 by bus through Honduras to El Salvador. Archbishop Romero, murdered a few weeks before while celebrating mass at the Divine Providence Hospital in San Salvador, was already buried; so were thirty people killed at his funeral at the Metropolitan Cathedral he refused to complete, his statement on behalf of the poor who now mourned him.

She knew she was moving into a bad situation, and wrote to her mother: "I have all sorts of reactions—from feeling robbed at not having had the opportunity to know Mons. Romero (we're to work in his diocese), to horror at the paranoia & fear of the right & their brutality, to wonder at the gospel message & the impact for acceptance or rejection that it has on people, to feeling with the poor of Salvador & their loss of someone whom they knew cared for them."

As Ita, and her friend and Maryknoll Sister Carla Piette, prayed about the Salvador they hoped to help save from imploding, prayed for the people whose lives they might salve with Christian charity, they knew that the death of Archbishop Romero signaled their own increasing involvements with the Cross of Christ. Her letter to her mother continued: "But we believe that his death will bear fruit—& it's part of the Christian mystery we celebrate this week—and in that same Christian tradition, we'll go to Salvador."

No matter that she was impelled to Salvador by belief, with hope, and because she loved the people there; she knew she had placed herself at risk. She wrote to her friends: "My timing couldn't be worse, I know—but this is the culmination of a process that started last August when the need was foreseen to reinforce the group there. Actually I'm still reeling from Romero's death—because we were supposed to work with him & in some way I guess I feel that part of my future was robbed."

The palpable disappointment at their arriving too late to work with Archbishop Romero continued in her letters: "In His own time the Lord got me here; although since His ways aren't ours, the journey wasn't all that clear at times." But the disappointment transformed itself into hope once she and Carla began to settle into El Salvador: "However, once getting here and having the chance to meet and talk with a number of people, I feel differently. It's a privilege to come to a Church of martyrs and people with a strong committed faith. Though I'm here only two and a half weeks, I have a very strong conviction that I'm where I should be—though the particulars of the future are not very clear yet."

Her words tumbled out of the spin dryer of Salvador: "...an incredible climate of violence....1102 assassinations....It boggles the mind." She continued, in a postcard to friends: "I've been very impressed with the pastoral agents I've met. Last weekend, I attended a course for rural liturgy leaders 'Celebrators of the Word.' There were 60 men participating, the majority farmers, and their testimonies were right out of the Acts of the Apostles. It's awe-inspiring & humbling to come into a church like this."

One can only wonder what an intelligence officer, American or Salvadoran, would make of that. Sixty male "pastoral agents" sounds like the cast of a thriller movie. Add an American or two, and the mix begins to look like a political brew, a steaming cauldron of insurgency ready to challenge the status quo. Too few intelligence officers understand the non-partisanship of Christianity, the extra-political stance of the Christian in the face of what can only be designated as evil. For Ita Ford, and surely for Carla

Piette and the other American missionaries in Salvador, the recognition was the same: "Historically this is not the ideal time to arrive on the scene—but the Lord got us here for some reason."

Finding work was both hard and easy. The Archdiocese of San Salvador identified the department of Chalatenango, in the north, as a priority for its ministry. Ita, the New Yorker, knew well the compactness of the city; rural Chalatenango was a different challenge. She wrote: "It's still a little difficult for me to get a framework around the rural situation—as you have several small towns and then scattered groupings of houses which make up a parish, as opposed to the concentration of people in a poblacion." Ita and Carla saw and weighed different options, different invitations. Some places were too isolated, some were too conflictive. They finally ended up in the city of Chalatenango, a major marketplace about an hour and three-quarters from San Salvador. The winter of Salvador was approaching, where "it often rains all night and sometimes there's a short cloud burst during the day. However, the only time I saw a thermometer, it said 96 degrees—so much for winter." The climate was wearing, the heat was explosive.

Within weeks she wrote to her sister that she was "supersaturated with horror stories and daily body counts....I'm not sure how you get 'acclimated' to a country that has an undeclared civil war going...." She also sent along the news that she and Carla had jobs—as workers of the emergency committee in the vicariate of Chalatenango: "What that means is that the church of San Salvador is facing reality & getting ready to help with food, medicines & refugee centers." The army, she explained, was in continual conflict with the various popular organizations that wanted to form a new government, causing people to be displaced, or flee in fear. American military aid was not offset by humanitarian aid. "I don't think we could have dreamed this job up before we came—but we came to help & this is what we're being asked to do....there's a lot of displaced people & disrupted lives—& that's what we'll be focusing on." It wasn't exactly a war. It was a slow and selective massacre.

Ita Ford knew full well what was going on in this country where there were fifty or one hundred assassinations a day: "It's really a complex situation—if only it were as simple as good guys vs. bad—but it's not. And a lot of groups don't have their act together & aren't in agreement about what to do & when. I think a lot of lives are lost that way."

Six months before she was murdered, Ita wrote passionately about the road before her: "I don't know if it is in spite of, or because of the horror, terror, evil, confusion, lawlessness—but I do know that it is right to be here...to walk in faith one day at a time with the Salvadorans along a road filled with obstacles, detours and sometimes washouts:—this seems to be what it means for us to be in El Salvador." The political horror-show displayed itself in the little town square of Chalatenango. Women would come to the Maryknoll Sisters: their husbands had disappeared. Ita would go to the authorities, quietly, to inquire. Every day, it seemed, with one or another of the women, Ita Ford knocked on an official door to ask a military officer about one more human life.

Reality never left her view: "…it really isn't the historical moment for unknown religious to pop into an area where many people are on the run, scared witless & caught in crossfire of the military, trying to wipe out training centers of the popular organizations." She wrote wryly of "the nightly shootings and the daily hearing tests. 'Did you hear that?' 'Yes.' One night I burst out laughing as well—'Yes, our ears all seem to be ok.'"

XI.

They ended up living within feet of a National Guard Barracks, and their activities were surely interpreted in the worst light. How must it have looked to Salvadoran military? Two North American women drop out of nowhere and suddenly, it would seem, they have established a headquarters for refugees (read "subversives" in the government lexicon). Somewhere in the whorls of American-Salvadoran intrigue the story evolved that Ita and Carla were knowingly running a "safe house," that their prayer and service were a front for political intrigue.

They were politically astute, but they were not political agents parachuted in by the revolutionary forces. Their deepest concerns were the meek and the poor, the women whose husbands had been "disappeared," the children for whom law and order was a rifle butt and a scowl. Their classified documents came from Matthew, Mark, Luke and John. Their classified materiel was rice and beans and mercy. They were not stupid; they recognized evil and they recognized what they were challenging.

So that they could visit the poor in the hills, Ita and Carla managed to obtain a second-hand jeep, which they called "Miss Piggy" in honor of its apparent ability to navigate some of the wetter roads. They had their own visitors as well. One Maryknoll Sister, Peggy Healy, became their "Washington commuter." She recalls sitting one evening in the place in which they lived, surrounded by piled-up sacks of food. Ita turned to her and deadpanned: "We're not going to get shot. We'll get killed by the damned food falling on us."

The quintessential New York attitude could help one survive in Salvador, but Salvador did not go away. The faces of Salvador captured Ita's mind and were engraved in her memory. She was convinced of the innocence of the young, and could not believe they were capable of what the military accused them of.

Once Ita went with a mother to identify the buried body of her son, and she spoke later of how those who buried him preserved his dignity even in death. When he was uncovered, there was a white cloth still protecting his face. She shared this recollection with Maryknoll Sister Madeline Dorsey, with whom she and Carla had lived near the coast in La Libertad from April until early June: how peaceful he seemed, how terrible his end, how dignified his burial.

He was perhaps the same youth she mentioned to her niece: "Yesterday I stood looking down at a 16 year old who had been killed a few hours earlier. I know a lot of kids even younger who are dead. This is a terrible time in El Salvador for youth. A lot of idealism and commitment is getting snuffed out here now."

The Salvadoran winter rains did not slow the deaths. In order to maintain some sense of sanity, to relieve the strain of the brutal realities they sought to salve, Ita and Carla often went to La Libertad, to meet with Madeline Dorsey and others to pray, to share a festive meal (if even at the local McDonald's), perhaps to see a movie. Their extended community enjoyed a population explosion when Maryknoll Sister Maura Clarke joined Madeline in August, bringing the ranks of Maryknoll Sisters in El Salvador at the time to five.

No one of them had any thought to be anywhere except in Salvador; each accepted her own situation as a part of the suffering of the people, and hoped their presence and their ministry would somehow balm the wounded populace. Ita never doubted: "Again, it's not a question of should we be here or not —but what does being in this situation call for in the way of response. It's trying to order a war situation in some way so you can keep sane and functioning."

The rains continued, and the fighting wore on. One afternoon, Ita and Carla were approached by a Salvadoran military officer from the nearby barracks. A young boy, perhaps sixteen, had been accused of collaborating with the guerrillas. The officer did not want to put him in the Salvadoran justice system, because nothing would ever happen; he did not want to keep him, because perhaps he might have to kill him; his only choice, he continued, was to give him to the Church.

Their aging jeep, "Miss Piggy," was pressed into service. Ita and Carla drove the boy and some others apparently released by the military toward their homes. They crossed the El Chapote River once, and again, as it wound its way across their path. On nearly the last of the multiple crossings the river suddenly burst into an angry swell, overturning the jeep. Ita recalled later she did not know how she got out, whether she had been pulled by the men, or pushed by Carla. She somehow bobbed down the river for two miles, thinking she would soon meet the Lord, until she grabbed the limb of a tree and pulled herself up, to spend the night in the field naked and alone, exhausted, relentlessly bitten by mosquitoes.

Carla was dead.

Ita selected the readings for the funeral, which she attended. She was nauseous, she was dehydrated, she was feverish, she was moving toward pneumonia. She ended up spending four days in the hospital.

The rushing river that overcame them and silenced one life, and the million mosquitoes left to harvest on the living, are metaphors for Salvador. The dark waves crashing out of the contorted politics of the country simply swallowed resistance and carried it away, either in death or to be chewed to pieces in life.

Ita's family grew apprehensive. She wrote to her mother: "I know this is a very hard time for you. I know that you're concerned and worried about the situation and I don't know really how to alleviate that. I truly believe that I should be here and I can't even tell you why. A couple of weeks ago Carla and I were praying and we both cried because it was so unclear to us why we were here, although we felt strongly we should be. Well, it's now quite clear for Carla, but I still have to keep asking to be shown. I can't tell you not to worry—that would be unnatural—it would be like someone saying to me—don't hurt because Carla died. In fact the last few days have been really hurting ones— probably because the shock of the whole thing—the event and to my system—is wearing off. All I can share with you is that God's palpable presence has never been more real ever since we came to Salvador—He's made a lot of things clear to us—what we should be doing, etc.—and I trust in that and I hope you can too."

She recovered, and she did not leave. Carla was dead and buried in Chalatenango with the poor; Maura Clarke came north from La Libertad to join Ita there.

The movements and the very mobility of the North Americans must have been suspicious to their military neighbors. What was Ita Ford doing boarding a long-distance bus on Saturday, September 13, 1980? She was going on retreat. What was Ita Ford doing flying to Nicaragua on November 24, 1980? She was going to a Maryknoll assembly. What was Ita Ford doing flying back to Salvador on December 2, 1980?

XII.

Numbers can only quantify. Ita reported to the Maryknoll assembly: "From January through October 1980, there have been twenty-eight assassinations of Church personnel, three woundings, twenty-one arrests, four profanations of the Eucharist, forty-one machine-gunnings of Church buildings, fourteen bombs, and thirty-three search and seizures of Church properties." It was Thanksgiving in Nicaragua and the Maryknollers celebrated, commiserated, questioned and prayed. Madeline Dorsey and Teresa Alexander had unsuccessfully tried to coordinate their flight back to El Salvador with that of Maura Clarke and Ita; in fact Madeline had telegraphed Ita in El Salvador with the suggestion.

The mail arrived at the parish house in Chalatenango the morning of December 2, 1980. Father Efrain Lopez received another threat, this time a letter. They had all been harassed before. The military harangued them, used its vehicles to block the church entrance. A little later the sacristan was pulled aside and shown a list of names. The killings, he was told, would begin that very day.

Shortly after 2:00 p.m. on December 2, Ursuline Sister Dorothy Kazel and Jean Donovan parked their white Toyota "Hiace" van in front of the main terminal at El Salvador's international airport. The Lanica flight from Nicaragua arrived at 2:30 p.m., with only Madeline and Teresa aboard. No problem, said Dorothy and Jean, they

would gladly return a few hours later for Ita and Maura,
who were booked on a COPA flight. Somewhere a radio
crackled, enough to be overheard or intercepted: "No, she
didn't arrive on this flight; we'll have to wait for the next."

The airport was both busy and tense that day;
Salvadoran National Guardsmen were making their presence known. On November 27, six leaders of the Revolutionary Democratic Front (FDR) had been abducted and
murdered—the 1993 United Nations Truth Commission
blamed Salvadoran security forces—and the funeral was to
be held the next day. While awaiting Ita and Maura in the
terminal, Dorothy and Jean ran into six Canadian nationals
who had arrived for the funeral. Within minutes, the
Canadians were stopped at a military checkpoint just outside the airport, but let go.

Sub-Sergeant Luis Antonio Colindres Aleman, a
twenty-four year old National Guardsman who earned 650
Colones a month and lived with his twenty-year-old girl-
friend in a barrio in Ahuachapan, was in charge of the airport detachment that day. He had been alerted to the first
airport visit of Dorothy and Jean; at about 6:00 p.m. he was
told they were back again. He ordered five Guardsmen to
wear civilian clothes, take their G-3 rifles, their gunbelts,
and their ammunition cases and to join him in their unit's
green jeep, which they had to jump start. They were, he
later testified, going out to get some gas.

This is what seems to have happened. At about 6:30
p.m. Sub-Sergeant Colindres Aleman changed into civilian
clothes and ordered five Guardsmen to do the same. With
the uniformed Guardsman who had come to the barracks

to report the return of Dorothy and Jean, they all rode in the National Guard jeep to the airport checkpoint. There he dropped off the uniformed Guardsman, with orders to stop all traffic except the missionaries' white Toyota van. Outside the airport, near the first toll house of the uncompleted toll road, Sub-Sergeant Colindres Aleman and the five others waited for the white van.

Twenty-five minutes later the white van arrived. They stopped it, interrogated the four women inside, and Sub-Sergeant Colindres Aleman ordered three of the Guardsmen to get into the van, one as driver. The two vehicles—the white van with three Guardsmen and the four women, and the green jeep with Colindres Aleman and two additional Guardsmen—proceeded toward El Rosario la Paz, stopping once to restart the jeep. At the National Guard command post at El Rosario la Paz, they stopped again, leaving the unreliable jeep with one of the five Guardsmen to watch it. Sub-Sergeant Colindres Aleman and now four National Guardsmen crowded into the white van and rode toward Zacatecoluca, then six kilometers on bumpy back roads toward San Pedro Nonualco, then even farther along a small dirt road. Then they stopped.

This is the testimony of National Guardsman Carlos Joaquin Contreras Palacios: "The place was uninhabited; they continued about three blocks; they stopped, and Colindres Aleman ordered the women out of the van, and then they raped them, after which Colindres Aleman ordered the Guardsmen to shoot to kill those four women, which they each did; the declarant noticed that Colindres Aleman's gun misfired, so he does not know if Colindres

Aleman actually shot the women; then Colindres Aleman explained that he had given this order because the women were guerrillas or subversives; after this the deponent and the others drove back in the van to El Rosario la Paz with both the interior lights and the radio on."

They had a replacement vehicle waiting at El Rosario la Paz. They took the white van toward La Libertad and set it afire with gasoline. Sub-Sergeant Colindres Aleman coordinated their transportation.

XIII.

Guadalupe Gomez Alfaro lives in San Francisco Hacienda, Santiago Nonualco. At about 10:30 on a Tuesday night early in December of 1980—he does not know the exact date—Gomez Alfaro heard a vehicle pass directly in front of his house. About ten minutes later he heard gunshots, then the same vehicle (from the sound of the engine) passed again in the opposite direction, toward the city. He heard no voices, no groans, no cries.

At 5:30 the next morning Gomez Alfaro went to milk the cows, and about fifty meters north of his house he saw the bodies of four women. He was afraid, and did not go too near them, but he could see that three were blindfolded, one with flowered cloth. Some clothes were near them. At 6:30 a.m. he passed again, and the bodies were still there. They were buried there at ten that morning; he heard that it was ordered by the Judge, but he does not know who buried them. Only later he heard that these were the four North American nuns.

The villagers had reported the finding of the bodies to the local Militia Commander, Jose Dolores Melendez, and soon after two National Guardsmen and three Civil Guardsmen arrived and ordered those gathered there to dig a grave. As the summer sun rose higher in the sky, the local Justice of the Peace, Juan Santos Ceron, authorized the burials of the four "unknowns."

Early on December 4, the news of the burial reached

the local parish priest, who told the Vicar of the San Vicente diocese, who passed the information along to the American Embassy. Father Paul Schindler, a part of the "Cleveland Team" of missionaries that included Dorothy Kazel and Jean Donovan, had already found the burned-out van on the road toward La Libertad. He suspected they were dead. He, too, learned from the parish priest where they were buried, and he was there that afternoon when United States Ambassador Robert White arrived. At the request of the Ambassador, and with permission of the Justice of the Peace, the women were disinterred. They had been stacked one on top of the other in their narrow grave. Ita, the smallest, was on the bottom.

Three days earlier, at the Maryknoll assembly in Nicaragua, Ita Ford had translated some of Archbishop Romero's words about being poor, about being with the poor; she read her translation at the closing prayer service: "Poverty is a force of liberation....It invites us not to fear persecution because believe me, brothers & sisters, he who is committed to the poor must run the same fate as the poor....And in El Salvador we know what the fate of the poor signifies—to disappear, be tortured, to be captive—& be found dead."

XIV.

Fourteen months earlier the Minister of Defense of El Salvador, General Jose Guillermo Garcia, had made known his negative opinion of the pastoral work of some women religious there. Archbishop Romero replied with an opinion of his own: a public condemnation of the Minister of Defense. It was no secret that the Salvadoran military, from top to bottom, despised the Church, from top to bottom. It was no secret that the National Guardsmen had used their Heckler and Koch 7.62mm G-3 rifles to still the senses of four sensitive women. It was no secret that five ordinary men from five ordinary villages in Salvador raped and murdered four unarmed women.

But somehow all the investigations, all the searching for evidence—for rifles, for fingerprints, for names—just did not seem to progress. Somehow things got slow. Then they got even slower. Despite the fact that President Jimmy Carter shut down the dollar spigot to El Salvador three days after the murders, somehow the Salvadoran military thought its own bureaucracy could stall and defeat the search. Perhaps the Americans would lose interest? Proper procedures can take a very long time in El Salvador.

There were two official Salvadoran investigations: a public government commission and a private National Guard investigation. The public commission was headed by Colonel Roberto Monterrosa, Director of the Armed Forces Studies Center. The private self-investigation by (and of) the Salvadoran National Guard was headed by Major Lizandro Zepeda Velasco, who reported to Colonel Carlos Eugenio Vides Casanova.

Five months after the murders, in April, 1981, the American Embassy identified the murderers and gave the names of all six Guardsmen to Defense Minister Garcia. Soon after, the FBI matched Colindres Aleman's thumbprint to one taken from the burned-out van. Perhaps he touched the van in the airport parking lot, he said. Guardsman Jose Roberto Moreno Canjura's weapon matched an expended shell found at the murder site. No, he said, he had not lost possession of his rifle, and he had nothing to do with the murders.

It was clear by then that justice would be slow in coming to El Salvador. The hydra-headed problem seemed to reduce to two points: First, how could a junior noncommissioned officer take five troops on such a mission without the explicit or implicit orders from those senior in their chain of command? Second, if those senior in the chain of command were complicit in the action, how could they direct or cooperate in an investigation that would ultimately end with themselves?

The same "system" that knew its own corruption and turned a budding guerrilla over to the Church, to Ita Ford, now looked to itself for the truth. Ita's comments had barely reached an American friend when the deaths exploded in the world media: "Salvador is distinct from Chile—more brutal, vengeful and lawless. Chile's repression always tried to have the facade of law; not here. No one bothers with such niceties."

It took a long time. Major Zepeda shared his information with Colonel Monterrossa. Within a few months, the investigations were ready to close, with no findings, despite the fact that each officer knew Colindres Aleman was directly responsible for the murders. One can only assume the problem lay—at least partly—in whoever was indirectly responsible for the murders.

Conclusions are hard to come by in any true bureaucracy. The activities of the families of the murdered women, of the Maryknoll Sisters, of members of the media, of so many others with such real and deep concern were fired by initial charges that they were "gun runners." They weren't just nuns, claimed then UN Ambassador Designate Jeane Kirkpatrick that December; no, indeed, said Secretary of State Alexander Haig the following March, they may have been running a roadblock. They believed what they said, but they were wrong. Disinformation and intelligence are such reflective undertakings that it is often impossible to separate impression from outright lie, especially as either moves up to the next higher official with increasing ratification.

The five National Guardsmen were finally accused of the murders and jailed in the spring of 1983. At that time, then Secretary of State George P. Schultz directed an "independent and high-level review of all the evidence available to the United States government pertaining to the churchwomen's case." New York Judge Harold R. Tyler, Jr. headed the investigation, which produced a 103-page document, "The Churchwomen Murders: A Report to the Secretary of State." The document is a trip into the heart of darkness, a look into "a society that seems to have lost its will to bring to justice those who commit serious crimes against it," a look into a military that "sought to shield from justice even those who commit the most atrocious crimes."

The Tyler Report concluded this: The facts were clear enough to show that Sub-Sergeant Colindres Aleman ordered the four National Guardsmen to rape and murder the four churchwomen. The facts were not clear enough to show that Sub-Sergeant Colindres Aleman acted, as he once claimed, on higher authority. The facts were never clear enough to answer why.

Colonel Monterrosa offered a political explanation to the Tyler Commission. He said that the churchwomen were probably subversives. As such, the military would have preferred them eliminated.

Colonel Carlos Eugenio Vides Casanova was commander of the Salvadoran National Guard in 1980. By the time of the trial, he was General Carlos Eugenio Vides Casanova, Minister of Defense. It is very hard to run an underfinanced military. In November, 1983, the U.S. Congress froze $19.4 million in aid to El Salvador pending (demanding?) accountability for the murders. Six months later the trial of the Guardsmen was held, May 23–24, 1984, before Judge Bernardo Rauda in Zacatecoluca. It ran nineteen hours, all through the steamy Salvadoran night. There was a lot of testimony. There was not much of a defense. At one point a defense attorney said, "If they did it, they did it on orders, because in the National Guard if someone does not obey an order of this type...." His thought melted into the night, unfinished.

At 4:15 a.m. Thursday, May 24, 1983 the following persons were convicted of homicide in the deaths of Ita Ford, 40, Maura Clarke, 49, Dorothy Kazel, 41, and Jean Donovan, 27: Luis Antonio Colindres Aleman, Carlos Joaquin Contreras Palacios, Francisco Orlando Contreras Recinos, Jose Roberto Moreno Canjura, Daniel Canales Ramirez. They were the first members of the military ever so convicted. They were sentenced to thirty years in prison.

They are still there. On November 5, 1988 a political amnesty was called for Salvador. They asked to be released; they were denied. The judge ruled that the murders were not a political crime and not covered by the amnesty.

In March, 1993, the United Nations issued the report of its Truth Commission, which determined that the five had indeed followed higher orders, that the whole event was planned in advance. It argued that Major Zepeda and Colonel Monterrosa and Colonel Vides Casanova each obstructed justice. It argued that the military knew what it was doing all along.

XV.

Sister Grace Myerjack is a member of the Maryknoll Cloister in Ossining, New York; she lives there with other contemplative Maryknoll Sisters. She had lived with Ita in St. Louis; she knew her well during Ita's 1978–1979 "Reflection Year." She was also close to Maura Clarke.

Grace spent the early part of the winter of 1980 in solitude. One night, in the seconds before full sleep enfolded her, she saw in her mind's eye both Ita and Maura. The face of Ita and the face of Maura were fully present to her, and they said one simple word: "Come."

They do not look like they are suffering, she said to herself. Why do they need me?

The memory is quite clear to her. They were not suffering. They were complete, they were full. They were who they were.

It was some days later when she heard.